# WILDLIFE
## IN THE
# KINGDOM
# COME

# WILDLIFE
## IN THE
# KINGDOM COME

### An Explorer Looks at the Critters and Creatures of the Theological Kingdom

## KEN C. JOHNSON
## JOHN H. COE

ZondervanPublishingHouse
*Academic andProfessionalBooks*
*Grand Rapids, Michigan*

*A Division of HarperCollinsPublishers*

*To my father and Timothy*

. . .

*To Greta, my friend*

Wildlife in the Kingdom Come
Copyright © 1993 by Ken C. Johnson and John H. Coe

Requests for information should be addressed to:
Zondervan Publishing House
Academic and Professional Books
Grand Rapids, Michigan 49530

Edited by Leonard George Goss and James E. Ruark
Interior design by James E. Ruark
Cover design: Ken C. Johnson and Jamison–Bell Advertising
Cover illustration: Ken C. Johnson and Fred Warter

Published in association with Sealy M. Yates, Literary Agent, Orange, California.

*Library of Congress Cataloging-in-Publication Data*

Johnson, Ken C.
    Wildlife in the kingdom come : an explorer looks at the critters and creatures of the theological kingdom / Ken C. Johnson and John H. Coe.
        p.  cm.
    Includes bibliographical references.
    ISBN 0-310-57681-4
    1. Theology, Doctrinal—Humor. 2. American wit and humor, Pictorial. I. Coe, John H. II. Title.
BT28.J58      1993                                                                    93-1464
230'.0207—dc20                                                                        CIP

Printed in the United States of America

93  94  95  96  97  98 / CH / 10  9  8  7  6  5  4  3  2  1

# Contents

# Preface

Whether or not you find it a credible claim, the little work you hold in your hands is indeed a theological dictionary . . . sort of. This effort, like its larger predecessors, aims to describe, define, and depict a variety of theological and philosophical terms. Unlike other dictionaries, however, its primary concern is to address the theological issues that occupy the majority of evangelical discussion and debate. Put another way, these are the notions we all at some time or other would gladly kill to defend or denounce! Thus, with polemics and passions raging all about, we thought that perhaps a different perspective from the traditional approach would help provide not only some objectivity, but a little more understanding as well. We determined that as dictionaries go, what is needed is a horse of a different color. And so this theological bestiary was born. (As a point of clarification, it did not, as some reviewers have suggested, "crawl out from under a rock.")

We began by vowing to disassociate ourselves from the unhealthy elements that can creep into certain kinds of slipshod scholarship—namely, guesswork, name-calling, and various forms of bitterness and envy. However, shortly after undertaking this enterprise we found the aforementioned elements indispensable. After a moment's reflection, we agreed to employ such means only—and we must emphasize this—only when the mood struck us.

Another exciting aspect of our findings pertains to the ancient Latin terms for each creature, which offer incredible insight into the origin of species. We hasten to add that although the type of Latin found here is not strictly speaking a "dead" language, many have suggested that it is gravely ill.

Perhaps one note on the semi-serious side is in order. In no way is the humorous approach taken here meant to demean or devalue the precious biblical truths that are essential to Christianity. Rather, our aim is to give perspective, insight, and yes, even a smile to the sincere yet frail theological constructs that Christians employ to express their faith.

We would like to offer a sincere word of thanks to a few people whose contributions were invaluable to this project. First, to our friend Sealy Yates, who enthusiastically introduced the project to Zondervan. Also to Stan Gundry, who had the vision (or was it blindness?) to publish and support this book. And a very special thanks is due our editor, Jim Ruark, who constantly encouraged, nurtured, and endured our efforts, feeble and always late as they were. And finally to those familiar-sounding authors found throughout the footnotes of the text: You have been our teachers, our tormenters, but above all, our inspiration.

# The Calvinist
## (Consumus Tulipius)

Along the mountain ranges known as the Protestant Peaks (formed by the enormous shifts caused in the Reformation circa A.D. 1520) dwell the dedicated herds of the Calvinist. Having migrated from the Roman regions on account of violent clashes with papal bulls, these staunch survivors flourished for centuries on a diet of Providence Posies, Polemic Poppies, and lush bunches of Theological Tulips. His species can be easily identified by its five-point rack of antlers, a remarkable feature most helpful to explorers attempting to locate the herds and track their migration to scriptural formations emphasizing (1) total depravity, (2) unconditional election, (3) the scope of the Atonement, (4) irresistible grace, and (5) perseverance of the saints.

Though at one time the Calvinist herds were vast, in recent years this creature is rumored to be on the brink of extinction. No doubt this is in part due to the repeated attacks by his natural enemies the Arminian and Liberal, as well as certain dispensationally inclined Fundamentalists and wily breeds of Pinnocks.[1] Some applaud this development and think the Calvinist's long-standing claim to being a select species is at an end. Yet many believe that as explorers discover more about these ancient creatures and their feeding habits, the Calvinist is somehow predestined to persevere.[2]

In the illustration opposite, we see emerging from the background the Calvinist's somewhat distant cousin, the Amyraldian. (Observe the four-point rack of antlers and expression of unlimited hope for atonement.) In the upper right corner appears the strict Hyper-Calvinist, whose points are often too numerous to count.

[1]For further reading on the Calvinist-Pinnock debate, see Clark P. Nock's *The Calvinist: You're So Vain, You Probably Think This Song Is About You,* also available on cassette and compact disc.

[2]An enthusiastic defense of the Calvinist is found in the bestseller *Getting the Points Across: Expansion of the Calvinist,* edited by J. I. Sacker and R. C. Sprawl, Flag of Fact Press.

# The Evangelical
## (Lostus as Lambus)

Throughout the lush Gospel Grasslands of the Protestant Expanse graze the ever-devout Evangelicals. Although the species has flourished for many centuries, it is the extremely large flocks of the last fifty years with which most explorers are familiar. Owing to clashes with various other species such as the Neoorthodox and even the Fundamentalist, much of the Evangelical's "abundant life" should have suffered. But despite their docile appearance and sometimes endless bleating, these once-lost lambs possess an incredible and instinctive obedience to their overseers.

Shepherds renowned for their great animal attraction have often gone to great lengths to house and protect their flocks. These efforts range from building Megachurch Barns to giant Crystal Corrals. The success of these settlements has resulted in a vast proliferation of instruction manuals and guidebooks detailing the rigors and rewards of maintaining a large flock.[1] A few shepherds have declined this form of ranching, however, preferring the more intimate confines of the local Stewardship Stable.

However, none of these measures has absolutely ensured the safety of these flocks. The most notable lapses in security have involved the well-worn (and still successful) method of some other species' camouflaging themselves as Evangelicals, entering the herd, and leading it to desolate regions near the Brink of Destruction.[2] These tragedies often occur due to the shepherd's own sheepish behavior or preoccupation with writing yet another instruction manual.

Given the hazards and pitfalls that have so often beset this group, one cannot help but observe their vast flocks with wonder. Though skeptics say otherwise, many believe the Evangelicals' ability to endure speaks of an unseen and tireless attendant, one whom some explorers call the Great Shepherd.

---

[1] For further reading on this subject, see Bill Highbell's *Meeting the Demands for Designer Stalls* and Shoeller's *Robert's Rules for Reaching the Unflocked*.

[2] Also known as a gathering place for various species of Philosophers and Televangelists.

# The Fundamentalist
### (Belt-us witha Biblas)

**W**ithin the rocky Reactionary Ravines in the heartland of the Protestant Prairies dwells the fierce and bellicose Fundamentalist. Ferocious for his size and reactive in nature, he preys upon packs of Darwinians, Higher Critics, and Social Gospel Gophers that migrated to this region in the nineteenth century. Although his basic instincts tend toward peace and harmony, these characteristics may often lie hidden beneath his defensive disposition. This protective posture has likely evolved from fending off numerous and savage attacks from a variety of natural enemies, including Left-winged Harpies, Pinko Packrats, and Cottonmouth Commies. And though these hostile conditions often provoke the Fundamentalist to wrath, he can exhibit extraordinary charity toward a variety of weaker species. Extreme examples of this marvelous and mysterious mingling are demonstrated in certain Fundamentalists' ability to "handle" snakes.

Researchers cite a particularly congenial coexistence with his neighbor, the Evangelical. This amenable association endured for several years until a new strain appeared on the horizon, namely, the Neoevangelical. By the 1950s, tensions between the Fundamentalist and this latest variety of Evangelical had erupted into full-blown hostilities. Licking their wounds, the Neoevangelicals soon migrated to the more moderate western coastal regions and the temperate Christianity Today Timberlands.[1] Since then, the Fundamentalist has exhibited extreme caution if not outright suspicion of all visitors to his rigidly constructed confines.[2]

Although some explorers have suggested that the Fundamentalist's days are numbered, reports of his revival abound. After all, no one can deny that this animal's survival is attributable to his steadfastness and . . . amazing grace.

---

[1]For further reading on the Fundamentalist-Neoevangelical wars, see Cal F. Henry's *Badgered to Death: A Neoevangelical Heads for Higher Ground.*

[2]More about the Fundamentalist's social habits can be found in David Huntem-Down's *Seduction of the American Prairies.*

# The Existentialist
## (Touchea Feelie)

**W**hile many explorers bustle about their daily routine with little time for reflection, the brooding visage of the melancholy Existentialist has brought many such expeditions to a thoughtful and even troubled impasse. Known to congregate primarily in isolated areas around the Isles of Authentic Existence, Existentialists are thought to be one of the more temperamental creatures in the theological lands. While typically scorning normal behavior and feeding patterns, they may exhibit bizarre traits in attempting to find their peculiar niche. Interestingly, this preoccupation with unconventional and individualistic behavior is often lost in their fashionable appetite for turtleneck sweaters, facial hair, and just about anything black. This contradictory behavior is further evident in the Existentialist's deep instinct to go it alone, while at the same time he may gladly "go it alone" in snooty cliques!

It is alleged that there are two species of Existentialist that share a number of traits yet differ in their overall orientation to feeding. One is drawn to the Meadows of Ultimate Concern, where he feeds on varieties of lush theological grasses. Therefore many have sought to classify him as a Christian Existentialist.[1] The other has developed a taste for ground insects and worms from the leaner Despairing Drylands and thus has been described as an Atheistic Existentialist.[2] The lack of nourishment available to this latter species makes him easy to distinguish from his somewhat overweight and overfed cousin (see illustration). However, whether there is any essential difference between these two is difficult to determine inasmuch as they often congregate at the same watering hole to commiserate over their misery.

When all is said and done, the Existentialist's somewhat unpredictable behavior and appetite for the "moment" greatly prohibits extensive and objective study of this species. As a result, theological explorers find this musing creature especially difficult to track. Perhaps this is for the best, for where the Existentialist's trail ultimately leads may be too hot for turtlenecks.

---

[1]For further reading on this variety, see Sorrie Quirkygaard's *Flights of Fancy and Other Leaps of Faith* and its companion volume, *Better Off With Blindfolds.*

[2]More reading on this variety appears in "Jumpin'" J. P. Sartre's *Blind Alleys, Dead Ends and Other Activities for Rainy-Day Fun.*

# The Heretic
## *(I-deni et Tu)*

**M**any centuries ago zealous (and at times, unbalanced) expeditions sought to rid the Great Primitivchurch Plains of a dreaded and poisonous parasite, the Heretic. Found throughout the theological lands, the Heretic is most fond of feeding off helpless herds of Unorthodox and Neoorthodox whose diet lacks any substantial dosages of doctrine or theological propositions. Although small and difficult to detect at first, the bite of this malicious little pest can have devastating results. As infection forms around the bite, schism and dissension spread throughout the body of the helpless victims. This condition ultimately gives way to such fatal diseases as Arianism, Modalism, Universalism, and the Ten-Percent Tithe.[1] In some cases the Heretic's bite has been noted to be so malignant as to infect and sicken even the Orthodox.

Whereas the ancient method of fire and brimstone was once considered the only sure means of coping with this insidious bug, today a more civilized approach is practiced, namely, the vicious spilling of ink. This method, however, frequently has little affect on the more tenacious members of the species. It may be that the only adequate measure in dealing with this group is to rekindle an old flame, that is, smoke 'em if you got 'em.

---

[1]Scholarship requires that we acknowledge that this last item is not in the strict sense associated with the Heretic. But some might suggest that in a theological sense this is "damned" annoying.

# The Problem Passage
## (Thornus-in-Ursidius)

Anyone wishing to explore the theological kingdom will inevitably encounter the Problem Passage. This terrifying creature roams the Theological Hillsides and creates extremely difficult going for the would-be traveler. By positioning himself stubbornly in the explorer's path, the Problem Passage impedes any attempt to forge a trail toward a complete theological system.

As vexing as this encounter may be, most explorers (at least those desiring respectability) do not retreat readily from the Problem Passage, but instead seek to hunt him down with hopes of an easy kill. Unfortunately, this brash tack has left many an adventurer trampled, bruised, and eager to find a more arms-length approach toward this ugly beast. One's options, however, are limited.

Some subtle explorers have chosen to reclassify this creature as belonging to a species known as an Anomaly. By doing so they either ignore it or attempt to render it harmless by promising to wrestle with it later. More experienced travelers have also resorted to the method of insisting that their present purposes allow them neither time nor space to deal with the creature here, so they go around him altogether. Although this tactic has proven helpful in a myriad of tough spots, it also has led to some unfortunate theological detours.

Typically the Problem Passage becomes undernourished and quite neglected in one's own expeditions. But you will soon discover that other travelers unsympathetic to your theological treks will nourish the beast back to health. Take heart, though. The positive side of the Problem Passage is that he also grazes in the opponent's path. In such cases you should encourage this member of the species to be "fruitful and multiply."[1]

---

[1]For a standard work on this subject, see Bernhard Ram's *Unleashing the Problem Passage: Using the Text to Vex.*

# The Redaction Critic
### (Editus Maximus)

Along the banks of the Scriptural Shores the ravenous Redaction Critic drifts slowly and undetected through the grassy reeds as he continually forges his way upstream. Considered by some to be a creature of above-average intelligence, the Critic seems to follow a never-ending urge to find the source and theological motivation of the Scriptural Sea. Equipped with an insatiable appetite, he feeds on Scriptural Formations (chiefly of the synoptic kind) that flourish along the banks of such tributaries as Lake Luke, the River of Mark, and the Matthew Marshes. His feeding grounds extend as far as the waters surrounding the Pentateuch Peninsula.

Explorers encountering this shrewd and carnivorous species disagree strongly in their reactions to the beast. While some share the Critic's drive to find the theological motivation of his feeding grounds, others feel that, though the creature has a rather large mouth, he has bitten off far more than he can chew.[1]

---

[1]For further reading on this debate, see Eye Howard Marshall and Robert Drygun's *Go Gator Go* and "Stormin' " Norman Geiser's somewhat polemical work, *Handbags, Belts and Boots: A Guide to Hunting Redactors*.

# The Dispensationalist
*(Literalus et Dallus)*

Of all the species to emerge from the wide-open Lone-Star Landscape, perhaps none has managed to wiggle his way into the spotlight as effectively as the determined Dispensationalist. Though observed in one form or the other for centuries, it was not until the famed Darby expedition in 1845 that the Dispensationalist became an object of intense study and debate. Of chief interest to explorers concerning this newer strain were his strange markings (or charts, as some have named them) and his various abdominal segments that many believe indicate his past, present, and future age.

Further study centered on the Scofield variety, which seemed to define the species beyond any other previous breed. Today almost all Dispensationalists bear at least some family resemblance to this variety.

Several particular traits must be evident for a bug to be truly classified as a Dispensationalist.[1] For instance, many insects feed off the Abundant Grace Grasslands of the New Testament Territory, but the Dispensationalist is primarily found feasting on the Premill Pollen that settles inside the Blessed Hope Blossoms of this region. He also has a particular fondness for Normal Hermeneutic Hibiscus and Literal-Israel Iris.

In recent times there is much controversy among experts on whether the Dispensationalist is undergoing an evolution. A few think that something new and exciting is emerging, perhaps a transitional species that bears certain resemblances to the Covenant Crawdad.[2] Others continue to insist that the Dispensationalist has walled himself within a cocoon of social indifference. Oh well, perhaps if he were a tapeworm his usefulness would be easier to measure.

---

[1]For an in-depth analysis of the Dispensationalist, see Charles Wirey's *Swallowing the Dispensationalist Hook, Line, and Sinker.*

[2]Robert L. Sosee's innovative work *The Worm Has Turned: A New Approach to the Dispensationalist* offers a sympathetic account of this new subspecies.

# The Orthodox
## (Belevit Ornot)

On the Great Primativchurch Plains that stretch across the Kingdom Come dwell the staunch Orthodox. Being of ancient origin, the Orthodox is considered the first domesticated creature who alone was capable of carrying the load of the faithful few travelers willing to settle in the Theological Frontiers.

Intense homesteading and border conflicts over the past two thousand years have produced a variety of breeds of Orthodox such as Reformed, Catholic, and Eastern Orthodox as well as some bizarre subspecies such as the Heterodox and Neoorthodox. Nevertheless, the original Orthodox is easy to spot on account of his wide, strong hooves, which provide stability on the shifting grounds that seasonally appear as a result of doctrinally hazardous rains. Notice also the Orthodox's busy tail, ideal for flicking off pests—though in fact they pose little threat except in cases of severe disease carriers such as the Unorthodox and the Heretic.

A number of attempts have been made to interbreed this bovine with his subspecies in an effort to increase the tolerance of the Orthodox. All attempts have proven futile because of his stubborn constitution, which prohibits a dilution of his original pure stock. Some experts believe this resistance is healthy for the species, but others insist that unless the Orthodox enlarge their breeding habits, they may not be able to withstand the currently changing intellectual climate.

Those who think that the Orthodox has completely outlived his usefulness do well to remember the proverb "Don't muzzle the ox lest he thrash you" (or something like that).

# The Unorthodox
## (I-deni et Mostlius)

Young explorers attempting to forge a trail across the humid theological Lowlands inevitably attract pesky swarms of annoying Unorthodox. Though named for his feeding patterns upon the herds of Orthodox, Neoorthodox, and Heterodox, this tenacious little insect has developed an appetite for almost all flesh. A brazened gadfly, the Unorthodox has taken to invading various camps and expeditions to create chaos among unsuspecting explorers. Although his bite can be fatal,[1] more often it produces less profound symptoms such as flighty notions, wagging tongue, and sometimes just plain being struck dumb.

Efforts to thwart these relentless swarms include the Schweitzer Swatter, Shoeller Spray, and even Barth-Be-Gone Bug Repellent. However, most of these remedies have enjoyed little success and may have rather negative side effects.[2] Seasoned travelers seem to have discovered nature's solution to this infestation. Their well-planned expeditions always include a team of Orthodox, who with a brush of the tail are capable of keeping these pests at bay. Conversely, travelers who place the burden of their exploration on the weaker Neoorthodox may discover that they indeed have a fly in their anointment.

[1]Cf. the Heretic.

[2]Some scholars have observed that explorers employing these ineffectual methods become disoriented and may wander off in search of Existentialist watering holes.

# The Neoorthodox
## (Bartis Beter)

Whenever a "new breed" appears on the theological horizon, many explorers rush excitedly to study and observe this unusual phenomenon. These expeditions do not always meet with great success, however. Such is the case, according to some, with the rather anemic Neoorthodox. Though ultimately determined to be a distant member of the Orthodox family, the Neoorthodox proved to have many features far less admirable than his great cousin. Of particular note are his bony legs and small hooves, which render him incapable of bearing the theological load typical of his ancestor.

Experts believe the Neoorthodox's dwarfed condition is the result of feeding upon the sparse doctrinal pastures indigenous to his native habitat, the Deutsche Drylands. Also common to most herds is their incapacity to stomach a strong diet of Propositional Truth, which is known to be a staple to the Orthodox and the Creed. Rather, the fastidious Neoorthodox typically feed off the wild weeds of Subjective Religious Experience that sprout throughout the drylands. As a result, numerous breeds have emerged, ranging from the slightly more sturdy Barthian to the emaciated and bizarre Tillichian (see insets).

Some explorers attempting to reclaim some practical purpose for this creature have sought to interbreed the Neoorthodox with the Orthodox. Most of these attempts have failed, though some have produced unusual hybrids of oversized brain capacity. Many experts suspect that these particular herds have migrated to Fuller Pastures.[1]

---

[1]For a romantic retelling of this migration, see Geoffrey Broomly's *Wagons West: New Cattle in the Upper Story*. More critical accounts are found in Harold Lindsail's *Where's the Beef? A Closer Look at the Neoorthodox* and Cal F. Henry's *Big Hat, No Cattle: A Saga of the Fuller Frontiers*.

*The Barthian*

*The Tillichian*
or "Ox Descending
a Staircase"

# The Textus Receptus
*(Speaketh Archaeus)*

Long ago in an age when the primitive shores of the Textual Critic Coastlands were forming, a fierce and tyrannical giant roamed the earth, the terrible Textus Receptus (TR). Rising from the Erasmus Manuscript Marshes, the TR ruled these lands particularly during the Jurassic Era of King James. Although at times his tenacious reign was disputed by such creatures as the Lachmann Lizard, for centuries he stalked this region unchallenged in his authority and authenticity. It was not until the arrival of the seemingly innocuous flocks of Wescott-Horts in the 1880s that his rule was seriously threatened. The advent of these strange birds created a tremendous imbalance among the inhabitants and explorers in this developing region. The dramatic shifts in the critical climate seemed to have a deadly affect on the once-mighty TR. His thunderous roar ceased, and quicker than you can say "Vaticanus," he began to disappear.

In certain camps, however, conservationists sought to preserve this endangered species. But by this time the region was consumed by bird enthusiasts who were set on the propagation of the winged Westcott-Horts. It was not long until the TR camps were overrun. Nevertheless, experts of these coastlands believe that the TR has been survived by his cousin, the Byzantine, a larger though more passive creature in nature.

Today there exist groups of TR fanatics who vigorously hold that he still rules these regions.[1] And though they cite many experts in support of their claims, perhaps the most remarkable appeal to authority is evident in the age-old claim, "If it's good enough for Paul and Silas, then it's good enough for me."

---

[1]For further reading on this debate, see Zane Hodge-Podge, *Lay Off My Lizard: The TR Defended,* and Bruce Netzger, *The Wescott-Horts: Proud Birds With a Golden Tale.*

# The Situationist
## *(Amori Ad Nauseum)*

In the intemperate forests of the Moral Mountains lives the flexible and accommodating Situationist. A chameleon at heart, he possesses the uncanny ability to alter his color (some experts say his moral stripe) to suit whatever ethical environment surrounds him. Subsequently, he is always testing the winds of doctrine and behavior to adjust accordingly. This trait in particular makes him an adept hunter of the Love-Bug, a creature indigenous to these woods that is his sole diet. Interestingly, this shifty creature also is endowed with peculiarly protruding eyes that can be focused (or unfocused, some would say) in all directions. This accounts for his alleged ability to see all sides of a situation. However, this trait does not always afford his small brain a correct outlook.

Owing to the Situationist's ever-changing instincts, explorers who attempt to study him are often frustrated when trying to determine the exact grounds he inhabits (although some suspect that he typically resides near the Shifting Sands). One thing is certain: The Situationist would not have us dispute the issue; rather, he might remind us that "all you need is Love-Bugs."[1]

---

[1]For further discussion on this creature, see "Maulin'" J. Montgomery and Joseph Letcher's *Situation Ethics: Sex, Lies and No Escape* and Montgomery's sequel, *Your Cheatin' Heart and Lying Eyes: Dissecting the Situationist*, also available on the Rhetoric Records label.

# The Agnostic
*(Noticia Dei Ignoramus)*

As the intrepid explorer makes his way in and around the Swamps of Skepticism, he will undoubtedly stir the incredulous croaking of the Agnostic. Dwelling in dark and cloudy waters, he produces a throaty bellow of indifference that often emanates to the far reaches of the theological kingdom.

In his early tadpole stage, the Agnostic feeds harmlessly on tiny Algae of Ignorance, Lack'a-Knowledge Lichen, and Suspended-Belief Beetles. However, this early innocuous form typically gives way to his highly specialized predatory behavior. His adult diet can range from Naive Gnats and Simple-Minded Spiders to the Non-Praying Mantis and Facetious Flies. Entangling these victims with his long, sticky, doubt-coated tongue, the Agnostic then numbs their vision with skeptic secretions. Soon thereafter the prey is consumed in the Agnostic's belly of unbelief.

Adding further confusion to his would-be prey is the Agnostic's uncanny ability to blend in with any surrounding notion. Also among his arsenal are his strong, muscular hind legs, which make him particularly adept at hopping over any intellectual obstacles that stand between him and his victim.

Many consider the Agnostic to be a nuisance and threat to explorers who pass through these swampy regions. This is very likely attributed to reports by some who, after handling this treacherous toad, have developed severe cases of wayward warts closely followed by fits of waffling and indecision. But by and large there is little to fear as long as you avoid the Agnostic's untamed tongue. Better yet, explorers would do well when entering these murky regions to pitch their tent far beyond the shadow of a Doubt.

As these regions are developed and the waters of the Skeptic Swamps recede, the extinction of the Agnostic becomes inevitable. This is perhaps fitting inasmuch as meeting his Maker will certainly wipe that dubious smirk off his face for good.

# The Demythologist
*(Nixxes Miraculous)*

Making his nest in several lofty regions of higher learning near the Academic Alps, the exploitive and determined Demythologist is often regarded by many to be merely an undesirable bird of prey. Circling above the fields of Scripture, this scary scavenger seeks out the supernatural herds of Texts. Upon spotting his prey the Demythologist swoops down with fierce determination, plucking the miraculous meat from the very bones of the herd. Returning again to his nest, the giant bird vainly claws over his meal in search of a morsel of existential meaning.

In the theological kingdom, opinions are quite divided about the usefulness of this bird. Some explorers applaud the feeding habits of the Demythologist, claiming they provide a clearer historical view of the scriptural landscape.[1] Others think his attacks mar the terrain so that even the most experienced explorer can no longer find the purpose or original meaning of the landscape. With this in mind, no doubt many traditional explorers would themselves enjoy carving up this bird for any festive occasion—an image that the Demythologist should well consider food for thought.

---

[1]For an enthusiastic defense of this bird, see Rudolfo Bult Mania's *Digging in the Dark: Stalking the Kingdom With the Demythologist.*

# The Premillennialist
## (Israelie is ur Babie)

Abounding in the woodlands of the Upper Eschatological Regions is the daring and high-flying Premillennialist. Soaring from one prophetic timber to the next, this amazing mammal dwells above the bustling affairs of the creatures below. His activities generally consist of gathering Prophecy Pralines and Second-Coming Seeds and an occasional Wallvoord Walnut. This practice is aided, of course, by the Premillennialist's uncanny ability to reach the loftiest vantage points in these regions and thus spot the events and sustenance that lie ahead.[1]

The Premillennialist rarely if ever associates with the lowly and entangled activities of the creatures in these woodlands. Rather, he seems intent on attending more heavenly and lofty matters. Because of this trait, some have claimed that he is of little earthly good and that his "pie-in-the-sky" approach to life is harmful to the theological environment.[2] Others counter that the Premillennialist's critics may be too harsh. They point to the dry, run-down conditions of these lands and claim that the Premillennialist's habitual gaze to heaven is actually a sign that this desolate region is due to be showered with a great reign—so great, in fact, that it will last one thousand years.[3]

[1]Much controversy exists over the ancestry of the Premillennialist. Some enthusiasts insist that he dates back to the Apostolic Era. Others believe that the first sightings were not made until the time of the Early Church Forest Fathers.

[2]For a critical history of the Premillennialist, see Doug Laughless Frank's *Less Than Losers*.

[3]A defense of the Premillennialist is found in Fiddley D. White Penta-Cost's *Looks Like Reign: Forecasting the Future With the Premillennialist* and his more popular work, *Here Come Some Things*. For a criticism of this position, see Oswald T. Alice's *Premillennialism: A Squirrelly Point of View*. Typically less criticism has been aimed at the Premillennialist's cousin, the Historic Premill, who some believe is less flighty and more willing to engage with his earthbound neighbors.

# The Proof-Text
*(Aceius-Intheholus)*

**P**erhaps the most welcome sight to many theological explorers in the rocky Pulpit Plateaus and Seminary Sierras is the magnificent and useful Proof-Text. Fierce, confident, and almost always grazing nearby, this beast of burden is consistently willing to bear the traveler's most precious tenets of doctrine as well as any flighty notions he may choose to espouse. This no doubt contributes to the animal's amazing reputation for agility and flexibility. Young explorers have found that these traits make the Proof-Text a very handy means to bolster one's ideas without having to risk the steep and slippery slopes that often surround most lofty propositions.

Although many explorers are extremely fond of the Proof-Text, a note of caution may be in order. Some have become attached to this species to the point that the spirit of true theological exploration is completely quenched. In such cases, the once-eager adventurer does no more than pitch his tent and exhibit his Proof-Text.

Oddly enough, other explorers sometimes find the Proof-Text unruly and vicious, confusing him with another species, the Problem Passage. This kind of confusion is not uncommon among the uninitiated, particularly in big game country. After all, one man's meat is often another man's poison.

# The Creed

*(U-Beter Belevit)*

As the sun slowly sets across the plateaus of the theological frontiers, the weary explorer may catch sight of the glorious herds of the noble Creed thundering across the Propositional Plains. Certainly as he is the most striking and preeminent of all the cloven creatures to roam these plains, it is startling to realize that the Creed at one time was threatened with extinction. Having emerged on these frontiers from such noble stock as the Chalcedon Cattle, Westminster Bovines, Belgic Bulls, and Heidelberg Heifers, the Creed would seem to have secured a permanent place on these prairies.

Early pioneers originally sought the Creed for his meaty substance, but then found his heavy, shaggy coat to be a great comfort against the icy winds of change. Ofttimes, however, the Creed was treated merely as game by callous and cruel Churchmen, who traded his hide to make a quick profit. Fortunately, the Creed's resilient offspring, the Catechism, found a welcome home among gentle shepherds from such diverse regions as the Franciscan Frontiers and the surrounding Reformed Reserves. However, other offspring such as the more obstinate Doctrinal Statement have become the focal point of numerous range wars that have broken out from time to time in these regions.

Although their herds have never returned to the greatness they once enjoyed, true explorers respect the Creed's lasting legacy. In fact, it may be said that any expedition that does not hold this beast in high regard is not worth a plug nickel.

# The Anathema
## (Alotta Excommunicata)

Although it is not the intent of this guide to prohibit or restrict the exploration of all areas of the theological kingdom, we are compelled to set forth a warning to those tempted to explore the Heretical Highlands and the neighboring Apostate Peaks. It is in these rocky regions where the dreaded Anathema dwells.[1] Being tenaciously territorial, he views all who enter his domain not as visitors but rather as . . . victims.

Those who have braved this terrain in hopes of retrieving wayward explorers have managed to collect bits of useful though somewhat gruesome data. For example, judging from the remains found in this wilderness, the primary diet of the Anathema consists of Liberals, Existentialists, Unorthodoxen, and Gnostics. These creatures—along with crazed and confused explorers who have attempted to build settlements here—serve as fodder in this God-forsaken place where the worm never dies. Research also reveals that the carcasses are always infested with Heretics, a further sign of the victims' defenseless state before death.

In many instances, animals such as the Orthodox, the Creed, and the Fundamentalist have driven their natural enemies into the lair of the Anathema. This strange occurrence is viewed by many experts as a type of "theological" natural selection.

Unfortunately, the Anathema's unusually aggressive attitude sometimes results in his leaping before he looks. This has led to a number of ill-fated accidents to smaller, innocuous animals who are naturally preyed upon by the less violent Rebuke, which resides on the borders of this region.

In the final analysis, the Anathema is no doubt the least likely candidate for a petting zoo. Consequently, every explorer would do well to remember that it is better to light one little candle than to face this curse in the dark.

---

[1]This creature was first sighted by the early pioneer Paul of Tarsus in the wilds near his Galatian outpost.

# The Talmud
## (Owl of Oy-Vey)

In the middle of the Intertestamental Timberlands bordering the humid Judaic Jungle lives the wise old Talmud. Renowned for his wit and wisdom, this sagacious bird feeds off local ground creatures such as Oral Traditions and Torah Interpretations that are abundant in these regions. The Babylonian and Palestinian Talmud are the two primary breeds (the latter pictured here), having evolved from their ancestors the Mishnah, the Halakoth, and the proverbial Haggada.

Although the Talmud is perhaps not an "inspired" species, theological travelers do well to observe this unusual creature very closely. Some believe that studying his habits and habitat are vital to understanding the nearby Gospel Glades, which the Talmud frequents.

Interestingly, some extremely gifted though perhaps eccentric experts on the Talmud—particularly of the Midrashic variety—have become a bit carried away with their research. Critics have concluded that these studies have mistaken this species, noble as it is, for a bird of a different feather that flocks together in the bordering Canon Country, particularly the Matthew Marshes.

A defense of this position is discussed in Robert Drygun's *Whoo! Is in the Matthew Marshes*, which some members of the Exploring and Tracking Society (ETS) have denounced as full of fowl ideas. Ultimately, this dispute may boil down to the old saying "a bird in the land is worth two critical books."

# The Fanatic
## (Un Tracus Minda)

The most colorful, lively, and easily identified inhabitant of the Social Works Woodlands is by far the frenzied Fanatic. Once firmly fixed on a Meaningful Cause Cottonwood or any other tree with a decent perch, this wild-eyed crusader embarks on a task that no neighboring tree-dweller and no explorer can ignore. While experts differ as to what drives him, it is quite clear that certain creatures initially benefitting from his efforts spur him on.

It is common knowledge that most animals native to the woodlands are unwilling or unable to maintain the Fanatic's fervent pecking pace. However, his remarkable and single-minded devotion inevitably stirs even the most tranquil tree inhabitants so that in a short time the activities in the forest reach fever pitch. Though explorers will want to approach this phenomenon with caution, they cannot help but be impressed with the Fanatic's zeal.

In many cases this admiration soon wears thin and typically gives way to resentment because the Fanatic, beset with frenzied activity, frequently drives his neighbors to frustration and fatigue. Where once many habitants worked and dwelled in harmony, now only the Fanatic and his frazzled faithful remain. Devoid of genuine devotees, the tree soon withers and fades. Eventually the rot forces out even the Fanatic, who, oblivious to the cause of it all, charges to the next tree. Unless the Fanatic's appetite is checked, it is likely that the once lush woodlands will become a wasteland, good only for wood, hay, and stubble.

The explorer, then, may face a tough choice when encountering this little pest: Cover your ears and move on, or . . . take careful aim.[1]

---

[1]For a technical and critical account of the Fanatic, see Franky Sheefer's *Addicted to Adrenalin: The Fanatic Dissected.*

# The Enlightenment
## (Pandorus Boxxes)

Across the sandy surface of the remote Rationalism Wasteland slithers the sophisticated and enticing Enlightenment. Having migrated in the eighteenth century from the Religion-Reigns Region, the Enlightenment's confident "stare-'em-down" pose soon intimidated the weaker-minded creatures of these lands.[1] While feeding upon tasty portions of Scientific Shrew Eggs, Reason Rodents, and Innate-Goodness Grasshoppers, this snake in the grass grew to great numbers, especially around the University Barrens.

Recently, however, the Enlightenment's dominance has been seriously challenged by hordes of invading Cultural Relativists, Deconstructionists, and Radical Feminists. Thus, not only is the Enlightenment's future survival uncertain, but also these fierce newcomers pose perhaps an even greater danger to theological explorers braving these wastelands.

Although the Enlightenment is perhaps not as poisonous as the infamous Garden-Variety Serpent, the general advice to travelers has been to avoid any contact with this endangered reptile. Some overly curious researchers have thrown caution to the wind only to fall under the spell of his hypnotic gaze. If he bites, the most notable symptoms in the victim are irreligious delirium and disbelief. The best antidote is still an old-fashioned shot of Belief Brandy mixed with crushed Religious-Defense Dandelions.

In spite of these dangers, it is yet unclear whether this deadly pest is more a nuisance than the predators that seek to replace him. It may be that future explorers are best advised to set fire to these drylands and give these inhabitants a taste of the Heat that is to come.[2]

---

[1]For a history of the Enlightenment's migration, see Vole Tair's sympathetic *Coils of Reason: A Trail of Rattles and Fangs.*

[2]A critical look at the contemporary Wastelands is found in Cal F. Henry's *The Firelight of a Barren Wasteland: Smoking Out the Enlightenment.*

# The Pelagian
### (Goodie Tu-shues)

By far the most beautiful and colorful of all the birds in the Moral Highgrounds is the proud Pelagian. This reigning king of pomp and splendor typically spreads his impeccable plumage for all to see. His feathered feat is usually an unabashed attempt to attract as many admirers as his flock can carry. So impressive is the sight that some have suggested that his brilliant display has a blinding affect on the admirers of this unfallen fowl.

The first bird of this kind sighted in the fourth century A.D. was considered unusually immaculate in presence and disposition. Many observers of that day were convinced that a diet of Sinless Sprouts and Freewill Fruit preserved his purity and innate innocence. However, as these lush fields of Good Deeds became scattered with the seeds of Total Depravity, the Pelagians were forced to migrate to higher grounds. Although the species flourished there for a time, soon droves of fierce Augustinians, feared for their Horns of Original Sin, pursued them nearly to extinction. Large herds of Scholastics and Great Reformers continued to flush these foul fledglings from their freewill folly.[1] With his immense train of propositional plumage sagging behind him, the Pelagian became easy prey, as he was never really capable of getting his ideas off the ground.

Although the Pelagian and his subspecies, the Semi-Pelagian, ultimately found safer havens among certain wilder varieties of Arminians, to most explorers his dazzling appearance seems to have lost its luster. Unless these plumed pilgrims recognize their fallen state, they have little hope of redemption.

---

[1]Seasoned explorers are measured by their ability to say this phrase fast ten times.

# The Westcott-Hort

## (Oldes is Bestus)

Amid the trees of the vast and arid Textual Critic Coastlands dwell the persistent Westcott-Hort. Always seen in pairs, these strange birds flourished from the end of the nineteenth century into the twentieth, particularly within the densely wooded MS (or Manuscript) Mountains. Interestingly, their massive flocking into these regions is largely responsible for the extinction of the Textus Receptus (TR).[1]

As to the peculiar behavior patterns of the Westcott-Hort, they exclusively nest in the species of trees known as Vaticanus (their favorite) and Sinaiticus,[2] both of which were originally classified as the Neutral Text Trees. Later these tall timbers came to be known as the great Alexandrians. In time, researchers determined that it was the ancient age of these mighty oaks that attracted these brainy birds. Further evidence showed that the Westcott-Hort are a peculiarly territorial species with regard to these Alexandrians. Thus they rarely if ever nest in the more abundant Byzantine, Western, and Caesarean trees indigenous to the MS Mountains. This nesting obsession is perhaps best demonstrated by the Westcott-Hort's uncanny ability to seek out one lonely Vaticanus sapling within a whole forest of Byzantine Birch and Western Willow.

While many find their strange fixations admirable, others criticize the Westcott-Hort's narrow bird's-eye view as responsible for their declining numbers. Conversely, the flocks of their cousin, the Eclectic, have grown in great proportions. And though these Eclectics differ in many ways, they have a similar instinct for nesting in the older Alexandrians. Mindful of this, resentful TR enthusiasts have made numerous efforts to have these timbers and everything associated with them reclassified as . . . saps.[3]

---

[1]For an insightful, evenhanded, and brilliant discussion of the demise of the TR, see the runaway bestseller by K. Johnson and J. Coe, *Wildlife in the Kingdom Come.*

[2]These are given the really profound nicknames B and **א**, respectively, by all the big-brained mucky-mucks.

[3]Although most technical guides are of little help to the novice explorer, the following readings may make the journey more enjoyable: Zane Hodge-Podge, *Westcott-Hort and Eclectic: Two Bird-Brain Approaches,* and D. A. Carlson, *The King James Brouhaha: Put a Sock in It.*

# The Postmillennialist
## (Bringus Utopius)

On the banks of the Millennial Lakes and Golden Age River dwells the industrious Postmillennialist. Unlike the Premillennialist and Amillennialist, he alone seems to possess instincts of any earthly good. This is particularly evident in his unique ability to fell Worldly Trees and transform them for the purpose of controlling the contaminated Streams of Modern Civilization.

The Postmillennialist's instincts affirm that, unlike some of his Eschatological neighbors, he is not afraid of a little hard work. As a result of his toil, his home is literally a haven from the natural decline that has settled in about him.

The Postmillennialist especially flourished during the Middle Ages and again in the romantic nineteenth century. During such times he fed off the Good-Deed Dogwoods and the Expanding Gospel Evergreens that were in abundance. However, the Great Wars significantly decreased their numbers. Many believe this was a result of the increase in Despairing Deadwood, Malevolent Mosses, and Pessimistic Parasites polluting the world's water supply.

Some experts of the Eschatological Regions lament the diminishing numbers of the Postmillennialist. After all, of all the creatures of these woodlands, at least the Postmillennialist gives a dam.[1]

[1]A positive account of the Postmillennialist is found in B. B. Warpath's *The Postmillennialist: Stemming the Tide in Troubled Waters*. For a celebration of the passing of the Postmillennialist, see Bruce Walkey's *Better They're Dead Than Read*.

# The Benediction
## (Blessus Dismissus)

With the end of each day the reflective traveler may be blessed to hear the low and melodious song of the Benediction. Known to nest primarily in the lofty timbers of the Highchurchlands, the Benediction can be found, though less frequently, in the nearby Lowchurchlands. Like his nesting habits, the song and appearance of this solemn bird seem to vary. Benedictions spotted in the Highlands, for example, are identified by a bizarre and pointy crown of color upon their heads. Their song is long, lofty, and somewhat monotone. Sadly, many explorers nod off before ever recording the entire melody. Instances like these encourage some restless researchers actually to sneak out of the Forest Cathedral lest they miss the competition of other species that usually begins with the pre-game ritual at 12:30 P.M. central time and kick-off at 1:00 P.M.[1]

Explorers who have studied the Lowland variety of this bird not only find his appearance more common (thus his nickname "Polly-ester"), but also have difficulty describing his song altogether. So low and lumbering is his melody that some confuse it with the rumble and growl of the Sermon. As a result, Lowland explorers rarely make it home in time for kick-off.

When all is said and done, however, the Benediction is truly a meaningful member of the theological kingdom, and any expedition that overlooks his presence really hasn't got a prayer.[2]

[1]Check your local listings.
[2]For a discussion of the recent attention given to the Highland variety of the Benediction, see Tom S. Howard's The Canterbury Trail: High Hats for Everyone.

# The Charismatic
## (Hebe-shebe-fizza-whazza)[1]

Any traveler familiar with the Glossolalia Glades in the Spirit-Baptism Outback has undoubtedly encountered its most populous resident, the carefree Charismatic. Having ancestral roots as distant as the Early Church Era, this creature is thought to have evolved from the Pentecostal, her wilder though ecclesiastically narrower parent. The reason for the Charismatic's emergence is unclear, though some research indicates this may be the result of the dead-'n-dry climate that has dominated the theological lands from time to time.

Of particular interest is the Charismatic's voracious appetite for Wonders-and-Signs Sprigs, Worship Wisteria, and Experiential Eucalyptus Leaves. These delicacies grow in abundance in the various "Vineyards" in which the Charismatic frequently forages. Some have also concluded that the nutrients in this diet equips the Charismatic with her legendary eyesight; thus her reputation for visions is unsurpassed. Experts further suggest that her feeding habits lend to the ecumenical company she keeps, particularly with creatures of the more sedate Episcopal and Anglican enclaves and the Catholic Renewal Coastlands. Still, it is generally agreed that Charismatics most often gather en masse around the Maranatha Moors and the Calvary Chapel Cliffs.

Supporters of this jolly jumper insist that she is a delightful addition to a land often filled with stuffed shirts.[2] Yet numerous experts of the Outback remain miffed and mystified at the rapid growth of the Charismatic population and are uncertain whether this is ultimately good for the theological ecosystem. They believe that the Charismatic's ecstatic bouncing is trampling all over the boundaries established by the Word-o'-God Rangers, who patrol and attempt to maintain order in the theological kingdom.[3] Regardless of this controversy, it is clear that there are enough hands held high on behalf of the Charismatic to keep her from going down under.

[1]No interpretation was available at the time of publication.

[2]For the positive account of the Charismatic, see John Windbur's *Holy Hoppers That Heal*.

[3]A critical view of this creature can be found in John MacArthy's *Leapin Loonies on the Loose: The Ungrounded Charismatic*.

# The Heilsgeschichte
## (Mabies Hass Rabies)

Emerging from the ashes of the Great World Wars in the desolate regions of the Deutsche Drylands is the humorous yet controversial Heilsgeschichte. Evolved from a truly noble ancestry,[1] this modernized and existential canine came to make his permanent home near the famous Fatherlands of Historical Criticism.

It is generally accepted that this perky pup possesses an especially sanguine nature on account of his diet of hearty Redemptive Roots. However, it is equally clear that his taste for German Critical Crazyweed has produced undesirable side effects. As a result, he lacks the more noble constitution and size of the orthodox strain, whose diet includes the nutritious Historical Hominy.

Overall, some theological explorers believe that the study of the Heilsgeschichte provides some experiential insight into these theological lands. Many others, however, think that any hound who displays such intense loyalties to the critical climate of the Fatherlands is a junkyard dog likely to be left outside the gate.[2]

---

[1]The Heilsgeschichte's larger and more noble parent, the Salvation History, can still be spotted around the Propositional Prairies that border the Drylands. This larger species feeds off not only Redemptive Roots, but also the hearty Historical Hominy (hence his name).

[2]The most definitive explanation of this beast is stated by Kaiser von Rad: *"Mein Kampf un Strudel der Spritzen on Donner und Blitzen"* in volume 2 of his *Dog Matikisch.* For a critical response, see Will Hengstenburg's *Das Hund ist ein Goon.*

# The Exegete
### (Minutiae et Mania)

Nestled beneath the surface of the Textual Terrain in the Seminary Savannas lives the never-tiring and prolific Exegete. Though akin to the larger Expository Sermon in his behavior, he surpasses all in attention to detail and eccentricity. He is rarely ever seen except by those experts or energetic novices willing to trek great distances to the Seminary region.

Most notable to the Exegete is his penchant for tunneling deep below the surface of the Textual Terrain. Aptly equipped with a singular instinct for digging, he makes his home in the solitary silence away from the bustle of the world above. Once settled, the Exegete spends most of his waking moments in search of the extremely illusive Meaty Meanings and scrumptious Subtle Minutiae, subterranean treats buried beyond the reach of less adept textual carnivores.

Numerous subspecies of Exegetes have appeared over recent centuries. Of all varieties, the Normal Interpretation Exegete is the most common and exacting in hunting behavior. One of the more colorful and controversial is the Existential Exegete, who exhibits a taste only for sweet Experiential Truths and Applications, which also live below the surface.[1] Some experts believe this type is currently growing in alarming proportions.[2]

Theological travelers seriously intent on understanding this creature are advised not to wait for the Exegete to surface, because this rarely occurs. One must go to his level, an experience that can be quite gratifying. Others believe, however, it is just downright suffocating.[3]

---

[1]For an in-depth account of this breed, see Rudolfo Bult Mania's biographical *Lost in the Text and Other Terrains: Tracking the Existential Exegete*.

[2]There have also been rare sightings of the Deconstructionist Exegete, whose behavior is so bizarre and obscure that there is much debate whether he should be classified as an Exegete at all.

[3]A positive account of the Exegete can be found in D. A. Carlson's *Getting Your Jollies With Exegetical Follies*, Finicky Publishers.

# The Presuppositionalist
*(Abundae Assumptus)*

Along the ledges of the immense and arid Apologetic Alps nests the noble and poignant Presuppositionalist. The most numerous breed, the Van Tilian, migrated from the Dutch Highlands, where dwell other similar but distinctive species such as the Bavinck Bird and the Dooyeweerd Duck. From his lofty perch, this Flying Dutchman preys upon ground animals of the Apologetic area, particularly upon Existential Ermine, Proof Possum, and the plentiful Ever-Digging Evidentialist. The Presuppositionalist, in turn, feeds this meat to his young as predigested starting points, assumptive analyses, and self-authenticating authority, all nutrients upon which they thrive.

Most scholars believe that the Presuppositionalist's ancestry goes back to the era of the Early Church Forest Fathers. However, there is a good deal of controversy whether he goes as far back as the Apostolic Age, as some affirm. And while controversy surrounds his alleged nesting in the Augustine Isle, clearly he flourished amid the Franciscan Forests, Bonaventura Flats, and parts of the Reformed Reserves.[1] Today Presuppositionalists flock in large numbers around the Westminster Mesas.

Though the Presuppositionalist is certain to survive, he is not without natural enemies. Numerous Freewill Foxes, Common-Ground Grizzlies, and Ligonier Lemurs seek out his nest to devour the bird, eggs and all. While such attacks are frequent, they are often unsatisfying inasmuch as many philosophical feeders find the Presuppositionalist a hard bird to swallow.[2]

---

[1] Much controversy surrounds these alleged early nestings of the Presuppositionalist in the Reformed Reserves, particularly around Geneva. Some experts believe these sightings were of a more hybrid breed. For a fuller discussion of this, see R. C. Sprawl and John Gushner's *Plucking the Feathers of the Presuppositionalist*.

[2] See John Framed and his popular account in *The Presuppositionalist: A High Flyer Whose Hope Is in Heaven*.

# The Annihilationist
## (Infirno-a-Nogo)

Amid the Contradiction Caverns along the shores of the Pollyanna Peninsula dwells the interesting but odd Annihilationist. A creature of ancient origin, he flourishes in cool and moderate climes conducive to long life and a quick and painless death. Consequently, he avoids at all costs the humid Eternal Torment Timberlands and the neighboring Great Lakes (of fire).

As with many other animals, there are two breeds of Annihilationist. The more populous Secular type lives in the most abominable and remote reaches of the Caverns, having a large appetite for No-Soul Stinkbugs, Materialism Mealworms, and That-Does-It Dung Beetles that thrive there.[1] The second variety, the Sensitive Annihilationist, feeds off No-Hell Gnats and Eternal-Bliss Termites, extremely rare insects that limit the population of this breed.

It is generally agreed that there is little value in studying the Secular variety of Annihilationist. Most believe this species should be left to the everlasting darkness it deserves. However, serious debate is presently raging within the conservative Exploring and Tracking Society (ETS) on whether the Sensitive variety should be studied and protected. While most can empathize with the Annihilationist's aversion to infernal suffering, his worried wing-flapping ultimately won't spare anyone the hot seat.[2]

---

[1]See the classic account of this secular variety in *The Party's Over: Analyzing the Annihilationist* by Eppi Curious and Thomas Hobbesnob.

[2]For a sympathetic treatment of this second breed, see John R. Nott's *Hell No, We Won't Go: A Case for the Annihilationist*. For a critical rejoinder to Nott, see Billy Greyham's *Bats in the Belfry: The Annihilationist on the Loose*.

# The Arminian
*(Choosis an Loosus)*

Perhaps the most populous of all creatures to roam the mountain ranges of the Protestant Peaks is the amiable Arminian. Unlike most of the other creatures in the Theocentric Woodlands, the Arminian's appearance and disposition seem shaped by an extraordinary relationship with human beings. This may be due to his preference for grazing in the Free-Will Farmlands. It is there that the Arminian struck an intimate acquaintance with the spiritual sharecroppers in the tract lands of Trent. Their fellowship remains unfallen ever since.

Further defining characteristics of the Arminian are his appetite for Resistible-Grace Grass, My-Choice Cherries, and Unlimited-Atonement Leaves. Some believe these paltry portions are largely responsible for his distaste of the more hearty Doctrinal Daffodils upon which the Calvinist regularly feeds.

Despite this criticism, the Arminian has flourished in the past few centuries contrary to his more staunch relative.[1] This is particularly evident in numerous breeds such as the Wesleyan, the Methodist, the Nazarene, and especially the free-spirited Pentecostal, which is unusually difficult to track.

In general, there is a good deal of controversy whether the Arminian and his numerous breeds will persevere. Some experts contend that the Arminian's poor diet and his unhealthy reliance on the goodness of mankind will surely bring about his demise.[2] Still others insist that although the Arminian species is not eternally secure, he alone has migrated to the glorious state of Perfection.[3]

---

[1]For a recent related text, see Clark P. Nock's *There's a Wideness That Won't Hurt Me* and S. Louis Johnson's critical response *There's a Gap in His Thinking*.

[2]A generally pessimistic view of the Arminian can be found in Roger NcKoll's *Free Will'in Phonies: The Tale of the Antiquated Arminian*.

[3]For a classic text on the Arminian (still in the original Latin), see Charles Finnee's *Willyawontcha Aintchagonna If-Icoaxya Wontchawanna*, Pleading Press Unlimited.

# The Mystic
## (Pious Most Hius)

Moving placidly among the madcap mania of the theological kingdom is the ever-introspective and misty-eyed Mystic. While living within the Experiential Enclaves and Transcendental Trees of the vast Devotional Desert, this spiritual species has become famous if not notorious for his unusual behavior. A nocturnal animal, the Mystic is forced to forage through many soul-searching journeys to the most secluded places, where he can find such rare rations as Mystical-Union Marigolds, Tranquillity Truffles, and Centering-Down Daffodils.

There are two primary breeds of Mystics, the first being the Orthodox Mystic, which is generally found throughout the wilds, particularly in the Catholic Coastlands and parts of the Protestant Peninsula.[1] The second variety, the Far Eastern Mystic, lives more on the edge of the wilds in the Wastelands of False Religion. His bizarre and astral means of travel so resemble the Gnostic that he has been considered by many an unpredictable mutation and therefore a freak of nature.

Today the Orthodox Mystic remains to a large degree an enigma.[2] Nevertheless, some explicit data have been gathered about his passive appearance. Equipped with his Nouwen Nose, Merton Mouth and Akempis Claws, the Mystic seems perfectly suited for his desert dwelling. Despite these features, critics insist that the Mystic's activities have little if any positive affect on the environment. They claim that no matter how inwardly active this creature is, his outward efforts are at a standstill.[3] Even so, one cannot help but admire a creature that diligently sojourns along the road less traveled.

---

[1] For a Protestant perspective on the Mystic, see Mad Madame Guyon's classic work *Shhh!* Sadly, many of her followers could not be "moved" to pick up this volume, much less read it.

[2] For a historical understanding of the Orthodox Mystic, see Theresa A. Villa's *Cuddly But Queer: The Mystics Are Here.*

[3] A somewhat critical analysis of the Mystic is found in David Huntem-Down's *Mystical Mating in the New Age and Other Wilderness Hanky-Panky.*

# The Joke
*(Corni Spherius)*

The wondrous nature of the theological kingdom provides for some rather strange cooperation among the various species. A prime example of unusual pairings is the jovial Joke and his trailing associate, the Sermon. Being a singularly frivolous and carefree creature, the Joke may precede and act as a sort of scout to the typically gruff and austere Sermon. In so doing, the Joke instinctively seeks to stir his surroundings to a lighter, more friendly atmosphere, thereby lulling the other occupants of the woods into a state of receptive ease.[1]

This jocular spirit, however, is short-lived because very soon thereafter follows the large, foreboding, and extended Sermon. There are cases of the Sermon's giving ground again to the Joke and even completely giving way to the creature altogether. This kind of intermingling is often very confusing to the explorer, who afterward may be overheard to observe, "That Sermon *was* a Joke."

One final note: Many Sermons, preferring to remain free of the disruptive nature of the Joke, choose to travel alone or with the more subdued species, the Illustration. Undeterred, the Joke will seek other companionship—perhaps the Televangelist.[2]

---

[1]For a lucid and positive account of the Joke, see Chuck Swingdoll's *Hammin' It Up in the Pulpit Prairies* and his very popular *Improving Your Punchline*.

[2]For a closer examination of the Televangelist, see "Pioneer" Pail Crouch's *Reaching Woodland Creatures . . . in a Funny Sorta Way*.

# The Topical Sermon
## (Shoutus Aboutus)

Amid the Gospel Glades that lie between the Teaching Timberlands and Pulpit Prairies lumbers the terrible and ferocious Topical Sermon. His bulky build and outgoing nature make him more conspicuous than his cousins, the Expository and Nonsensical Sermons. In particular, the Topical's large mouth produces a booming roar capable of intimidating or captivating any congregation upon which he preys. Thus he is far more likely than his cousins to encounter masses of Evangelicals and even feisty Fundamentalists.

This bully beast is not only fiercer than his cousins but more aware of his environment. Equipped with an acute sense of smell, he sniffs out any shift in the emotional winds that blow through his natural habitat. Sensing a change in the environment, he instinctively adjusts his behavior accordingly. This adaptive ability sometimes creates an uncanny communication with the inhabitants of these woodlands. Then again, sometimes the critters just sorta skedaddle.

When under control, the Topical Sermon is one of the more daunting and dignified of all the creatures in these parts. However, at times he can become so carried away in frenzied behavior that his otherwise noble demeanor gives way to a crazed and reckless disposition. All of this huffing and puffing aside, the Topical Sermon is most effective when he is able to sink his theological teeth into his task.

A curious natural phenomenon has taken place among various breeds of this species. Apparently observers have found that Sermons of this variety are almost always followed by a strange and emotional little creature classified as *Jus Asus i Amus*, or as it is commonly known, the Altar Call.[1]

---

[1]For further reading on the Topical Sermon, see W. A. Creezwell's introductory but useful text *The Topical Sermon: Exploring Pulpits With Tooth and Claw*, Rhetoric Press. A more popular discussion of this species is found in Chuck Swingdoll's *Lobbing Your Love: The Tender Topical Sermon*, Maudlin Press.

# The Expository Sermon
## (Long-n-dri Windius)

In the heartland of the Teaching Timberlands that border the Pulpit Prairies thrives the ever-stoic and staunch Expository Sermon. Though less daunting and spirited than his cousin, the Topical Sermon, this meticulous creature is an instinctive digger and a study in discipline.

The Expository's acute capacity for sniffing out details is particularly evident in his keenly penetrating search for meaty morsels of meanings within the surrounding Textual Trees. However, his narrow feeding habits prevent him from developing the energetic ways and large bulky muscles of the Topical variety. More detailed studies have suggested that the Expository's punchless presence may be owing to a lack of Homiletic Honey in his feeding. Yet some explorers defend the Expository's appetite on the grounds that of all the species of Sermons, he alone has a rightly divided diet.

Whatever the reason for his deliberate delivery, the Expository has been known to give way to an almost savage "textbook" display of power.[1] These instances of scratching with tooth and nail to uncover a meaningful meal clearly explain his stout and formidable constitution.

Such displays, however, may be the exception and not the rule. As many explorers will attest, the Expository Sermon typically plods along through these woodlands without interruption. This monotonous meandering may, in fact, make him a creature about which too much information is available—and unavoidable. Overcome by data, some explorers have abandoned their research of this animal and have sought a species more suitable to their temperament, namely, the Church Skit.

---

[1]For an enthusiastic account of the Expository, see James McGrowley Boyce's *Expository Sermons: The Only Way to Growl*, Picky-uny Press.

# The Nonsensical Sermon
### (*Absurdium Non-sequitur*)

One of the most unusual and playful of all creatures to inhabit the Pulpit Prairies is the Nonsensical Sermon. Unlike his larger relatives, the Topical and Expository, this wily beast exhibits inscrutable behavior that is singularly difficult to track. Because of his rascally disposition, some have likened their encounters with this beast to a three-ring circus. Such analogies are appropriate, given that the Nonsensical's primary instinct seems to be to entertain.

Consider, for example, how the Nonsensical Sermon dances around the Meadows of Meaningful Thought yet never stops there for nourishment. Or observe how he jumps through various hoops of Hysteria with tremendous dexterity, even though research has determined that he is quite unbalanced.

While such outlandish behavior is well suited for the bright lights of the Big Top, the Nonsensical Sermon seems ill-equipped to fend for himself in the wilds. Among certain extreme varieties, it is not uncommon to find this species begging for handouts from any explorer he may encounter. In exchange, of course, he will perform any number of his well-worn tricks. Yet, when these methods fail, he is not above pilfering from nearby church campgrounds.[1]

Despite his clumsiness, the Nonsensical Sermon has managed to populate a large part of the Pulpit Prairies. This expanse is no doubt owing to the dazzling effects their antics have upon a growing segment of naive expeditions. While the intentions of these explorers may be otherwise, they are unwittingly contributing to the overall decline of the Sermon species. Some studies also show an ominous rise in Heretic infestations among certain of these carefree critters.[2]

While even the most serious explorer is at times amused by this burly bozo, the overall effect of the Nonsensical's clowning is considered a liability. Some have suggested that if he insists on a circus-like atmosphere, perhaps his next stunt should involve being shot out of—or by—a canon.

---

[1]An example of these episodes can be found in Robert Tiltown's *Who Cares, Feed the Bears.*

[2]For an interesting account of this development, see Benny Hen-Peck's grizzly account *Good Night, Nurse* and his more recent work *The Annoying.*

# The Abominable Q
## (*Abit av Astretchus*)

Hidden among the rocky enclaves of the arid and snow-lined Higher Critical Himalayas lurks the legend of the Abominable Q. Much mystery surrounds his existence, and claims of his appearance remain extremely controversial. Although experts generally agree that no concrete evidence exists, a number of more liberal-minded explorers are determined to get at the source of this folklore. They believe that their findings are more than sufficient reason for postulating his existence.[1]

For instance, numerous unidentifiable tracks have been discovered alongside the remains of various Matthew mountain goats, Lukan llamas, and Harmonization hedgehogs, all of whom Q is supposed to be particularly fond. Furthermore, various sightings of a strange creature have been made by inhabitants of the nearby Source Criticism Community. But the contradictory nature of these reports leads many to believe that they are entirely unreliable.

As a result, many experts of these rocky regions seriously doubt whether there are any hard data surrounding the existence of Q. Researchers of an even more conservative scientific stripe find such conjectures incredible, pernicious, and downright abominable (hence his name).[2] By contrast, a growing number of experienced explorers are coming to believe that whether or not Q exists, there is no reason to fear him. They submit that the evidence for Q—such as it is—suggests a creature who is at most innocuous and therefore of no serious threat to the welfare of the community.[3]

The debate will likely rage on. After all, the average explorer seems to have a penchant for putting his Bigfoot in his mouth.

---

[1]Perhaps the most exhaustive research to date that includes incredulous eyewitness testimony has been done by the more liberal-minded Sir John Robinsome of Claremont in his sensational work *Hair-raising Hikes in the Critical Himalayas*.

[2]For a skeptical treatment of the legends surrounding Q, see the Dean of Defense at Lord-It-Over'em College, Robert Thommas's *Tall Tales From the Source Criticism Community*.

[3]For this irenic and perhaps balanced view, see George E. Porgy Lad's *Putting Q in the Zoo*.

# The Conscience
## (Inspectus Correctus)

Every theological traveler of background and breeding eventually discovers the provoking and at times irksome Conscience. A fellow famous for restraint, the Conscience instinctively latches onto explorers in all climates and regions. Yet because of his appetite for Understanding Sage, Truthful Twigs, and Self-Reflecting Rye, most explorers believe he can be of great help.

Once attached to an expedition, the well-trained Conscience will instinctively respond to any danger or approaching predator. Thus the weary traveler is alerted whenever immoral mammals or sinful snakes are nearby. Conversely, a peaceful Conscience is very likely a trustworthy sign that all is well and one can proceed without fear of danger.

But problems can accompany the Conscience. First, some travelers' Consciences are so quiet that they can hardly be heard at all. Second, many cases have been recorded of mutant and unhealthy breeds of Conscience such as the Narrow, Neurotic, Morbid, Doubting, and Calloused varieties. On the shoulder of an explorer, these deviants can send all kinds of wrong signals, resulting in serious harm to person and company.

Despite any unpleasant potential, reputable explorers agree that the Conscience is an inexpendable part of exploration. Witness the fate of some unscrupulous travelers who, after having their Conscience seared, are left to stumble their way through a world of Honest Johns.[1]

---

[1]For an interesting study of the Conscience, see *The Conscience: Puritan Prescription for Pinocchio and Other Blockheads* by Richard Backster. A more skeptical approach can be found in *Raiding the Conscience and Other Pests* by the famed exterminator Sigmund Fraud.

# The Problem of Evil
## (Scumm-us Among-us)

*Having made camp just after sunset, I built a small fire to fend off the encroaching cold of the cruel night. At length I set about to record the events of the day in my journal. No sooner had I taken pen in hand than I became aware of a presence in the darkness just beyond the everdimming light of my fire. Straining to detect the source of my rising anxiety, I was suddenly gripped with an overwhelming sense of terror and dread. In an instant, the sinister thing was upon me, sliding about like a dark misshapened silhouette. Beyond all fear and above all wickedness it seemed to whisper every imaginable, irreconcilable evil, all the while engulfing me in its foul and rancid breath. A moment later, a noxious rush of wind extinguished the last flicker of light from my fire—and with it I felt went all hope.*

Such is the record of one intrepid explorer's encounter with the Problem of Evil.[1] Yet savage attacks such as these are inevitable if adventurers are to be exposed to the other, wonderful wildlife indigenous to the territory of Theology Proper, where this wild beast resides. These vicious assaults have caused many to doubt whether the theological journey is all that beneficial.

Those who disdain theological exploration cite this beast as one of the primary reasons for abandoning the quest. They complain that if the Kingdom Come is indeed the promised land, how could such a creature be allowed to roam freely? "Is there no Overseer in these regions to protect its inhabitants?" they ask. "If so, why did he allow the monster to enter these lands in the first place?" Whereas some find these questions overwhelming, others consider them foolish. After all, where were these inquisitors when this land was formed?[2]

Many sage and experienced travelers have tracked the Problem of Evil in hopes of answering these and other disquieting questions.[3] And though these quests have presented few solutions, they have provided some insight. By dissecting tissue recovered from this dreaded beast, researchers have discovered a creature that is truly bad to the bone.

---

[1]Excerpted from the disturbing accounts of famed explorer Joseph Conraid's *Bladder of Blackness*.

[2]For a fuller discussion of this, see Job's *Anybody Get the License Number of That Truck?* Woe Is Me Press.

[3]See Dr. Augustine's classic work *The Problem of Evil: Look at the Size of That Booger*.

# The Evidentialist
## (Empericus Maximus)

Eventually every resourceful theological traveler will venture into the arid Apologetic Alps, which border the expansive Philosophical Plateaus. Here each explorer finds both difficult terrain and a true test of how well his expedition is equipped. This challenge is particularly formidable, for here lies the treacherous Mount Epistemology.[1] With its steep and slippery logical slopes and vast unverified valleys, this mountain has claimed many explorers who have lost their way and have been buried beneath a landslide of skepticism.

Though such dangers may prohibit the flourishing of many creatures in this area, the energetic Evidentialist seems well suited to the rugged terrain. Some attribute his success to a diet of Precious Proofs and Flavorful Facts that abound in this area. His constant digging for these scrumptious finds makes the Evidentialist a difficult target for the avalanche of problems typically associated with this region. It is against such conditions that the Evidentialist has stock-piled vast amounts of Tangible Treats to sustain him year-round.

Although some admire this amassing method, others are more skeptical. Most notably, the persevering Presuppositionalist—the other dominant inhabitant of this region—finds the Evidentialist's ceaseless burrowing misguided and disruptive. Faced with an ever-increasing number of digs and discarded finds, the Presuppositionalist has become a natural enemy of the Evidentialist and his fact-finding frenzies.[2]

Many who come to study the Evidentialist's habitat benefit from the show-and-tell traits of this industrious digger. However, it is still uncertain whether his methods bring a better understanding of the mount under which he dwells. Ultimately each explorer will have to decide for himself if indeed "seeing is believing."[3]

---

[1] For an in-depth discussion of this mountain and various expeditions made to it, see E. Manuel Cant's *A Rough-and-Ready Guide to Ascending the Knowls*.

[2] A more critical view of the Evidentialist can be found in "Snorin'" Jordon Clark's *The Evidentialist: Daydream Believer*.

[3] For further reading on the Evidentialist, see "Maulin'" J. Montgomery's *What Are Ya Blind? The Evidentialist Explained*. A more popular account is found in Gosh McTrowel's *That's a Fact, Jack!* and its sequel, *More Facts for Jack*.

# The Apocrypha
### (Maccabies If u Pleas)

Since the beginning of the Primitivchurch Era, much controversy exists among theological travelers regarding the nature and habitat of the unusual and imitative Apocrypha. Early records attest that Roman explorers made numerous sightings of them on the large Canonical Continent. Early pioneer Dr. Augustine accepted these as genuine at the famous Carthage Zoological Conference (A.D. 397) despite some opposition from his renown colleague Dr. Jerome.[1] It wasn't until much later, however, that certain Reformed researchers seriously questioned the reliability of these sightings. They stated that the Apocrypha's natural dwelling lies in the smaller Intertestamental Timberlands. Thus they believed that the Apocrypha was a mere mimic of the genuine species that inhabit the Canon.[2]

Research reveals that the Apocrypha itself has no less than twelve peculiar and distinct breeds, ranging from the less maligned Maccabees and Tobit to the zany Bel-and-the-Dragon. The fact that this species feeds on such plants as Prayer-for-the-Dead Daisies and Works-Righteousness Weeds—flora unknown to the Canonical Continent—is evidence to many that the Apocrypha is indeed a chimp of cheap imitation.

However, some critics have perhaps overreacted to the Apocrypha's doctrinally abusive feeding habits by ignoring him altogether. This seems a bit harsh. After all, the Apocrypha's antics may provide some useful insights into the Gospel Glades and the Old Testament Terrains that border his home. Take care, though. Spending too much time with this peculiar primate may garner you a reputation as a monkey's uncle.

---

[1]For an interesting historical account that favors the Roman sightings, see the findings of the Sixteenth Annual Meeting of the Council of Tridentine Enthusiasts.

[2]A more critical history of the Apocrypha is found in Martin Luter's *The Apocrypha: More Monkey Business From the Papal Palace.*

# The Radical Feminist
## (Nailus the Maleus)

**A**lthough cloaked in a curvacious black body of feminine poise, the Radical Feminist is in fact one of the most feared creatures in the theological kingdom. Suspended only by a slender thread of civility, this long-legged lady calls no man master. Rather, her world is a web of dominance and determination spun from years of bitter abuse and submission.[1]

A strict carnivore, the Radical Feminist has a particular taste for Superior-Male Slugs, Patriarchal Pill Bugs, and Philandering Fruit Flies, all of which easily become entangled in her web of wild aspiration. Mentally numbed by the noxious, emotion-filled fluid of her fierce pincers, the Radical Feminist's victims are soon drained of their traditional-role juices.

Perhaps the most bizarre aspect of the Radical Feminist's appetite is her overwhelming instinct to devour her male counterpart. While many believe that these are malicious males deserving their fate, others find this deadly embrace a sure sign of the Feminist's fiendish goals. Further study suggests that in some cases this treacherous trait has led to an unnatural occurrence among her species commonly referred to as a "less-being relationship."

Today a growing number of schools of higher exploration have taken a tremendous interest in the Radical Feminist. Enamored by her rebellious beauty, they feel that the impact of her bite can finally neutralize the ancient order of the animal kingdom.[2] However, her critics contend that despite the hard knocks that history has dealt her kind, the Radical Feminist has adopted an ugly method of reprisal, namely, hate male.[3]

---

[1]For a positive account of the Radical Feminist, see Gloria Stingmen's historical piece *Billboard Bondage to Business Boardrooms: The Elated Evolution of the Radical Feminist*.

[2]A recent sympathetic account of the Not-So-Radical Feminist is Patty Drygun and Elvia McKillson's technical work *Just the Right Bite: A Sociobiological Account of the Christian Feminist*.

[3]For a somewhat critical look, see Dr. James Dobsome's scholarly work *The Radical Feminist: Feeding on the Family*.

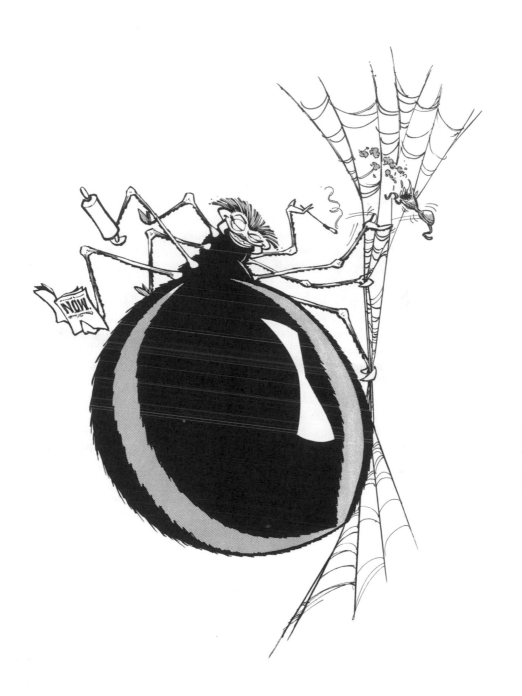

# The Gnostic
## (Ghostest witha Mostus)

Some years ago, while trekking the wilds of the Soul Journey Jungle, certain explorers stumbled upon the high-flying and double-minded Gnostic. Though they considered the discovery to be the dawn of a New Age, research soon revealed that this was merely an ape of ancient origin. Nonetheless, many explorers continued to go bananas over this apparent king of soul swingers.

Much of the uproar over this low-brow baboon concerns the notion that he is the missing link to the yet uncharted Knolls of Knowledge. However, experts are sharply split over whether the Gnostic has ever ascended to those lofty places. Most are unconvinced that this furry free-spirit sheds any light on the darkness around him. Rather, they point to certain varieties of Gnostics that engage in all manner of lewd and licentious monkey business. This fact, coupled with the animal's seemingly endless preoccupation with baubles, crystals, and other cheap trinkets, makes any claim of knowledge surrounding the Gnostic laughable. Interestingly, some older species do display a remarkable trait that requires them literally to shed their skin. This phenomenon is an apparent attempt to rid them of all worldly infestation. But all such ascetic attempts don't stand a ghost of a chance with these chubby chimps.

Finally, there may be some truth to the ridiculous claim that Gnostics never actually die. Ironically, even if they do, some misguided explorers always find a way to resurrect them.[1]

---

[1]For an interesting and perhaps enthusiastic account of alleged sightings and flourishings of the Gnostic in the Charismatic Coastlands, Psychology Savannas, and Designer-Church Domain, see John MacArthy's recent work *They're Here, They're There, They're Everywhere* and its sequel, *I Told You So.*

# The Ad Hominem
*(Shoottas From Hippus)*

To those who venture into the rough waters of the Seminary Seas, perhaps no image is more alarming than the daunting dorsal fin of the dreadful Ad Hominem.

Of its two main breeds, the Ad Hominem Abusive is the most relentless and brutal. This fiendish fish preys primarily upon swimmers wearing little or no outer arguments. Once the "attack against the man" commences, the jagged jaws of this ruthless aggressor tear through the undeveloped defense of the unwary explorer. Frequently the panicked victim thrashes about madly, desperately attempting to reach a buoy to support his battered and bloody integrity. Excited all the more by the victim's squirming, a feeding frenzy ensues as one Ad Hominem after another partakes in this savage assassination of character. Finally, with all ideas of escape exhausted, the tattered remains of the explorer's reputation drifts lifelessly with the current. Meanwhile, the insatiable Ad Hominem prowls the vast ocean of ideology in search of yet another victim.

The other most noted variety of sarcastic sea predators is the Ad Hominem Circumstantial. He often feeds in even greater regions than his cousin and is capable of swallowing his victim's background whole.

The sea explorer may take several measures to avoid these man-eaters. First, steer clear of the waters surrounding the Pulpit Peninsula, where the Ad Hominem often feeds. Second, remain well within the Reefs of Reason, an area incredibly dense with Proof-and-Soundness Seaweed, in which the Ad Hominem is liable to become helplessly entangled.

In general, the Ad Hominem can be quite enticing. With his "look-who's-talking" teeth and his "sez-you" style, his appeal to the theological novice has not gone unnoticed. But keep in mind: Anyone who goes fishing for an Ad Hominem is bound to catch a blowfish.

# The Liberal
## (Offa Deep-endus)

Of all the creatures in the Kingdom Come, none is of more proud and austere stock than the lanky Liberal. Found primarily in the tree-covered Steppes of Scholarly Endeavors, this long-legged creature flourished during the Enlightenment Era (circa A.D. 1700) when numerous subspecies emerged such as the Renans, the Ritschels, and the most interesting Schleiermachers. The Renans migrated to the northern highlands of the Historical Quest, where they were last sighted by the great traveler and classifier Dr. Albert "Your-quest-is-as-good-as-mine" Schweitzer, who believed them to be extinct. The other breeds continued for some centuries to dominate the steppes, particularly the arid Anthropocentric Region and the nearby Brotherhood of Man Bay.

The most notable of the giant's physical features is the long neck, which allows the Liberal to lunch on the Fruit of Moral Goodness and other high notions that grow atop the Trees of Enlightened Thought. Explorers who consider the Liberal a menace take a special interest in his diet as well as his long throat. They often express hope that this combination will cause him to choke.

Liberals have been classified by explorers into several subspecies, the most familiar of which are the various Pulpiteers and Academics. These varieties often exert their dominion over this region by stretching their sinewy necks upward, jutting out their jaws, and wagging their heads intensely. Many who believe this gesture denotes rank pride subsequently have redoubled their efforts to cut the heady herds down to size.

Whereas the classical Liberal herds were once numerous, in time they became quite sparse. Much ink has been spilled by experts in speculation as to the cause. Most scholars agree that during the great World Wars the Liberal's holier-than-thou habitat suffered extensive damage. As a result, the Fruit of Moral Goodness became so scarce that it could no longer sustain him.

Today a new breed of Liberal thrives in the theological kingdom, feeding upon vast resources of Higher Critical Camellias and Political Petunias (which, by the way, always lean to the left). In spite of his elitist tendencies, most explorers cheerfully acknowledge that they like the Liberal . . . particularly when served well done.

# The Pretribulationist
*(Adversities is-not Formies)*

Perhaps the most excitable resident of the vast Premillennial Plains is the perky Pretribulationist. Having feathered a temporal nest, he seems determined to roost well away from the Wrath to Come. This instinct to fly the coop may be the result of his large appetite for Rapture Roots, Tribulation Twigs, and Second Coming Seeds.

Despite his seemingly escapist tendencies, the Pretribulationist has shown a remarkable instinct for breeding, a trait researchers have termed "proselytizing."[1] This populous pastime is most evident in the pecking order of the Lone Star Leghorns and the Western Conservative Game Hens.

Perhaps because of his vast numbers and common appearance, the Pretribulationist does not attract the attention he once did. Recently his "sky-is-falling" cluck and "you've-been-left-behind" look seem to have lost their luster. Whatever the response, this is one bird that doesn't intend to be fried *or* tried by fire.[2]

---

[1]For a positive account of the Pretribulationist, see Hal Linseed's popular book *The Late Great Chicken Coop*. A more technical work is Lewis Spary Cheefer's *Out of the Frying Pan and Also the Fire*.

[2]A critical account of the Pretribulationist can be found in J. Barton Pain's *The Pretribulationist: Make Like an Egg and Beat It*.

# The Theonomist
*(Laedownius De Laus)*
also classified under
*(Charltonas Hestonius)*

Although novice explorers spend much of their time in the vast Faith Forests and the neighboring New Testament Terrain, few appreciate the wilds of the bordering Torah Territory as much as its peculiar occupant, the Theonomist. Due to the territory's sparse population, the Theonomist often feeds upon a steady diet of juicy Antinomians and Evangelicals who stray from their bordering lands into his realm (which is also called the Dominion Desert).

Whereas most creatures of the wilds respect the natural and long-standing boundaries between territories, not so the Theonomist. He stalks the NT Terrain as freely as the Torah. However, he has been generally unsuccessful in his attempts at pursuing his prey into the Dens of Discontinuity. This seems to have discouraged him from making any significant expansion of his actual borders.

The few native creatures of the Torah enjoy relative peace with the Theonomist only as long as they do not disrupt his domain. Instances have been recorded of prides of Theonomists messily devouring residents masquerading as other species while mating out of season.

The Theonomist's "letter of the Law" approach to life has hindered many animals living on the borders of the Faith Forests from migrating into this sparsely populated area. Nevertheless, a few have been lured. They imagine this territory, though now young and undeveloped, to be one day quite lush under the Theonomist's absolute reign and promise of harmonious order. However, others cite the infighting among the Theonomists as evidence against this.[1]

Overall, the Theonomist's attempts to expand his feeding grounds have been met with indifference, except in the case of a few skirmishes with mainline Calvinists and Evangelicals indigenous to the bordering regions. Nevertheless, his aggressive tendencies have made some feel he is a beast to be reckoned with. Perhaps. But the explorer may have less reason to fear the Theonomist than the piles of books he must wade through just to understand him.

---

[1]For a critical account of the Theonomist, see Fern Poythrus's *Hot Air From the North* and its companion volume, *That Looney Rushdoony*.

# The Moderate
### (Bothe Sideus Nowe)

Travelers who have a particular interest in bird-watching may find the adaptive Moderate a difficult species to classify. Because she is not indigenous to any specific doctrinal terrain or intellectual climate, her nesting place is not always easily sighted. Geographically we do know, however, that she makes her home somewhere between the Far Leftlands and Extreme Right regions. But because the chasm between these two points is so immense, explorers are still left with quite an obstacle in locating the Moderate's exact position. This suits the Moderate just fine inasmuch as being aligned to any specific area runs counter to her broad-minded nature.

Audubon enthusiasts who have tramped through the lowlands of the Extreme Right region have reported no sightings of the illusive Moderate. Rather, they found this area to be tenaciously defended by its lone occupant, the extremely territorial Fundamentalist—and they have the bite marks to prove it. Expeditions to the Far Leftlands have netted better results. Inhabitants of this area such as the Libertine Lark and the Freethinking Fowl seem to make this a more suitable place to feather one's nest. Nonetheless, experts inform us that the Moderate is incapable of surviving on a diet limited to Mere Morality and Filet of Sole Ethics, which make up the total food supply in this land.

Although many explorers still debate the success of the Moderate's search for a balanced diet, one ironic fact has emerged. The creatures existing on either side of her have discovered that she makes for a rather tasty meal. Such would seem to be the fate of a bird-brain who ultimately builds her nest on a fence.[1]

---

[1]A critical account of the Moderate can be found in Harold Lindsail's *Battle for the Barnyard*.

# The Antinomian
## (DeClawus deLawus)

Roaming with abandon beyond the borders of the vast Torah Territory is the free-spirited and wily Antinomian. Of all the creatures in the theological lands, he is renown for his vagabond instincts that lead him to live without any heed to natural law and order. These easy-going tendencies allow explorers frequent access to study (and in some cases to adopt) this unscrupulous scamp's behavior.

In many instances the Antinomian will boldly enter an encampment in search of a morsel of adventure or reckless ration. He is particularly fond of expeditions that pack any variety of wine, women, and song—preferably all three.[1]

For many, the independent Antinomian's carefree manner makes him one of the more charming creatures in this territory. However, the novice traveler should be alert to developing a personal affinity toward this clever little libertine. Although his spontaneity is quite appealing, his unprincipled behavior is entirely unpredictable and makes him completely untrustworthy. Abandon all hope of domesticating such a creature who is a law unto himself. After all, nature has veiled him with a mask, not as a beauty mark but rather as a warning.[2]

[1]It should not come as a surprise to the seasoned traveler that such wanton explorations exist. For further reading, see U. Gene Scot's *Lighten Up, You #@*%!!*

[2]For a critical account of the Antinomian, see Roofus Rush Dooney's *Roasting Raccoons Along the Torah Trail*, Lawful Press Unlimited.

# The Thomist
## (Aquinas Es Fineis)

It is generally accepted that there is no larger or staid beast in the theological kingdom than the tremendous Thomist. Notice immediately his massive size, evidence of an appetite that is unequaled in the Scholastic Seas. There, along the vast and deep Summa Shores and Catholic Coastlands he feeds on whole schools of Biblical Barracuda, Aristotelian Albacore, and Augustinian Angelfish, a seemingly impossible combination to digest.

Unfortunately, the Thomist's overwhelming size has intimidated many would-be explorers from entering these rough waters altogether. Some travelers flatly denounce these depths as hazardous to belief formation and consumption. They claim that a philosophical fish no matter how it's cooked is indigestible and foul.

Until recently, schools of Thomists had been hunted and destroyed by friend and foe alike of the Kingdom Come. Where once these beasts ruled the seas during the Medieval Age, they have become all but extinct, surviving in small pockets along the Jesuit and Dominican Reefs.

However, the past few years have witnessed a resurgence of these great marine mammals as well as an interest in the Scholastic Seas. In fact, there is evidence that even a few explorers from the Reformed Reefs have determined to make a life study of the Thomist. Their hope is that such research will unlock some of the secrets to the nature and origin of other species in the theological kingdom.[1] Nevertheless, many others are convinced that these waters are too polluted to be of any value. They believe that beneath the blubber of this bloated beast is nothing more than a whale of a fish story.[2]

[1]For an enthusiastic defense of studying the Thomist, see Pete Kreef's popular *Snorkeling in the Scholastic Seas*. See also Jack Maritain's more technical work, *Dissecting Tons of Thomism Along the Catholic Coastlands*.

[2]A more skeptical view of the Thomist can be found in Lorrain Bettner's old but useful work *Harpooning the Thomist: Providence's Pronouncement on All Papal-Plankton Lovers*.

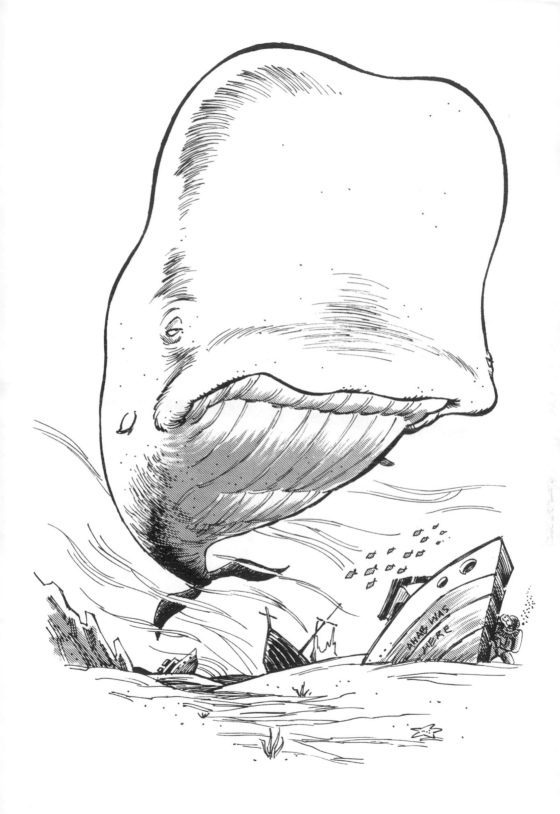

# The Process Thought
*(Sliddus Withe Tidus)*

Along the ancient shores of the Pantheistic Peninsula surrounded by the immense Philosophical Sea drifts the ever-changing Process Thought. Having evolved from the ancient Plotinus species, this more fluid fellow eventually migrated to regions containing other schools of intellectual and cold-blooded sea creatures. There the Process Thought feeds upon the exotic flora of Relative Rockweed, Finite Fungi, and Mutable Moss. This unusual diet makes him well suited to the radically changing tides of the sea.

The early dominant varieties of Process Thought came to be known as the notorious Whitehead and Hartshorne. Interestingly, a unique Cobb strain has recently been discovered in great numbers and size around the Claremont Cove, where all sorts of bizarre creatures tend to flourish.

Explorers should be on the lookout when they sink to the depths of the Process Thought. Despite his innocuous appearance and lack of theological backbone, this vacillating creature is in fact a true man-of-war. His noxious sting of slipshod thinking can be mind-bending and even fatal. Some believe that this explains the now classic and perhaps tragic case of noted explorer Clark P. Nock.[1]

Specialists in theological sea exploration advise that the only sure way to handle the poisonous Process Thought is to beach him. Such a task, however, is easier said than done, considering that no creature is more difficult to get a handle on than one that's lost its grip.[2]

---

[1]For his part, Clark P. Nock says he feels fine.

[2]For an alarming investigation into the dangers of the Process Thought, see John Fineburg's *Willy-Nilly Jelly Bellies: The Process Thought Revealed.*

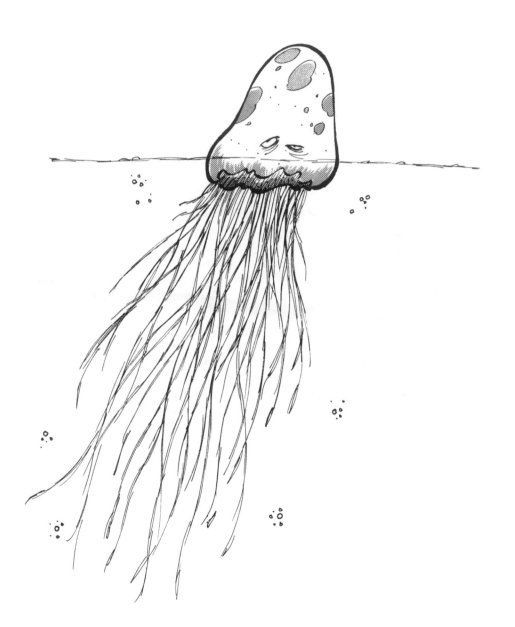

# The Monastic
## (Fattus Outta the Friar)

**B**y far the most retiring and elusive creatures in the lofty ranges of the Meditation Mountains are the solitary Monastics. First spotted in the Patristic Desert, they subsequently migrated throughout the high peaks located in the vast Roman regions. The Monastic's reclusive life and devotion to solitude make it difficult to locate him along well-traveled paths.[1] However, patient explorers hoping to catch a glimpse of this shy little fellow may find a small measure of success by observing various Rosary Bushes, Holy Grail Grottoes, and Veneration Vineyards.

Some observers have noted that unlike other creatures, it is not what the Monastic does but what he does *not* do that makes him of particular interest. For example, he takes no mate and no mammon and in some cases may never make a sound. This dainty and demure disposition has caused some critics to accuse him of being A–ssisi. Moreover, in the neighboring Protestant Peaks, some inhabitants have observed with skepticism the seemingly endless self-denials by which the Monastics strive to *save* themselves. Still others insist that these papal paupers have instinctively renounced their predatory nature and so have become padres of peace.

Whereas some animals travel in herds, flocks, or packs, Monastics always move "in mass." And although explorers may differ on the usefulness of this collection of critters, perhaps the debate is best summarized in the Latin expression *Myfather-canplaydominoes-better-than-yourfather-canplaydominoes.*

[1]Some sightings have been made along Abbey Road by St. Jude.

# The Cultist
*(Dictatus Degradus)*

Close to the blackened banks of the River of False Religion swims the truth-twisting Cultist. The legendary fierceness of this prodigious species is known throughout the theological lands and should be especially noted by inexperienced travelers—for though this creature usually feeds off fellow fish in these oppressive waters, his carnivorous appetite knows no bounds.

Typically attacking en masse, the group depends for its success on the health of the victim. Alert subjects are often able to ward off such attacks with a sturdy sound-teaching stick. However, theologically weak victims that emit a scent of low self-esteem are quickly consumed by schools of vicious devotees.

Though the larger leaders of these schools are generally classified as Sociopaths, their family includes a great number of less harmful but fanatical followers. As a result, a strong pecking order exists that requires strict adherence. Those who get out of line are severely punished and fed upon by fellow fish. Often the only means of scattering these savage scavengers is to filet their fearless leader. However, this may result in a phenomenon known as "martyrdom," a condition that will likely serve to increase the Cultist's numbers. Thus the theological novice should be alert to the fact that few Cultists are easily drawn away from their attachment to the school. Researchers have discovered that one successful method of re-programming is to net and transport these brainwashed bass to more civil waters.[1]

In recent years a number of the Cultist's distant relatives have invaded some of the more traditional waters. To the dismay of some (but surprise of none), these include certain species of Mega-Pastors and the ever-appealing Christian-Star Fish.

[1]For an excellent survey of these murky waters and their inhabitants, see Walter Marten's *Dominion of the Dolts*.

# The Posttribulationist

*(Sustainus Thruthe Painius)*

In the Salvation Savannas of the Premillennial Woodlands roams the small and protective Posttribulationist. Unlike the populous Pretribulationist, this creature is willing to endure the extremes of climate and the fierce predators that are present in these parts. In particular, his unusually bony and defensive outer armor makes him perfectly suited to take whatever pounding providence permits.

What accounts for the Posttribulationist's defensive frame is his insatiable appetite for large portions of Fortitude Fireworms, Martyrdom Mealybugs, and various types of Perseverance Plants indigenous to this area. Such a hearty diet prepares this feisty fatalist to suffer all the hardships that may one day confront him.

Experts who defend the Posttribulationist's "take-it-all-on-the-chin" approach insist his survival may depend on his commitment to hang tough.[1] By contrast, numerous critics believe that this "grin-and-bear-it" instinct is simply misguided grandstanding.[2] They cite evidence that in the final analysis there are only two types of species, the Quick and the Dead. Undaunted, the Posttribulationist strives to create a third subspecies, the Slow Survivor.

[1] For a positive appraisal of this creature, see Dougless Moo's classic *No Pain, No Gain: Pleading the Case of the Posttribulationist*, Survivor's Press.

[2] A somewhat critical assessment is found in John Wallboard's *The Posttribulationist: A Dumb-Dumb of the Wrath to Come*, Grace Unlimited Publishers.

# The Secular Humanist
## (Idid-it Meiway)

One of the most familiar creatures inhabiting the Wastelands of the arid Atheistic area is the sensuous Secular Humanist. An optimist at heart, he most enjoys the simple pleasures of eating, drinking, and whatever else appeals to his palate. Although this joy-monger wallows in large portions of Pleasure-Now Pears and Pagan Sugarplums, he also gobbles great bunches of Anthropocentric Apples, Inherently-Good Greens, and Sweet Potatoes of Scientism. As a result of this mixed diet, he typically grows to unusually large proportions and must spend most of his adult life seeking to satisfy his sinful sensations.

His enormous size intimidates many potential predators, yet the Secular Humanist is not without his natural enemies. This is especially evident in his defiant encounters with fierce breeds of Protective Protestants and Catholics that occasionally enter these dry regions. And though the Secular Humanist is willing to defend his territory aggressively from such unwanted outsiders, he prefers the simple serenity of rolling in the murky mire of man-centered marvels. It should be noted that certain members of the species have taken a whole-hog approach to invading other lands, particularly the Political Prairies and even the Schoolboard Badlands.

Whereas some explorers find the Secular Humanist's jovial and amusing appearance attractive, critics believe he is nothing more than a sophisticated slob. They maintain that the only useful purpose for this ham is on rye.[1]

---

[1]For a positive account of the Secular Humanist, see Aldous Huxter's *Brave New Bacon*, Godless Press. For a more critical view, see Jerry Fallwall's *The Secular Humanist: Pigs-in-a-Blanket*, Liberty Luncheon Publications.

# The Amillennialist
## (Millennia Within-Ya)

Although he is the most common inhabitant of the Eschatological Region, the shy and somewhat spooky Amillennialist is not an easy creature to apprehend. An ancient species of noble ancestry, he attracts little attention today compared with his Premill and Postmill cousins. This condition is probably owing to his colorless appearance and the inability of some experts to provide any "literal" data concerning his behavior.[1]

Some facts have emerged from research of the Amillennialist. For example, he is instinctively repulsed by the vegetation of the Premillennial Woodlands. This may be a result of the immense undergrowth of Rapture Roots and Tribulation Trees that flourish there. He seems to prefer, instead, the flora of the vast Reformed Forest and immense Roman Reserves. Some suggest that his omnivorous appetite for local Theologies of various color and stripe explains the wide variety of locales in which he dwells.

While considered by most a *spirited* creature, the Amillennialist avoids the toils associated with the Postmill. Rather, he adopts a "so-be-it" posture when confronted with the declining conditions around him. He is not, however, above being threatened.

Perhaps the most feared predator of the Amillennialist is the exacting Ezekiel Eagle. This precise bird of prey "literally" pursues the Amill from his perch in the distant knolls of Normal Interpretation bordering the Old Testament Terrain.

Explorers who study the records of the Amillennialist's lofty and elusive past are faced with a formidable task, for as they pore over numerous texts written about him, they must, it seems, read between the lines (see illustration).[2]

---

[1]For a positive and contemporary discussion of the Amillennialist, see Ant'ny Hokeyma's *I Found My Thrill With That Lil' Amill.*

[2]Historic Premill enthusiast George E. Porgy Lad counters the proponents of the Amillennialist in his classic work *The Amill as Roadkill.*

# The Revivalist
## (Seekius Soulis)

**W**hen traveling the Pulpit Trails of the lush Rejuvenation Jungle, no explorer can ignore the alarming cries from the sometimes rash but always ready Revivalist. Aroused by surrounding stagnation or any severe drop in the spiritual climate, this high-spirited creature is driven to reform declining conditions. Researchers attribute this instinct in part to his healthy diet of Get-Right-With-God Grapes and Turn-or-Burn Bananas.[1] Some also have observed that the Revivalist often stirs the slumbering woodland residents in the pre-dawn hours. Experts label these episodes "Great Awakenings."[2]

In many cases the Revivalist's intentions meet with a positive response. Numerous beneficial and healing movements in these jungles are the direct result of his labor and lungs. At other times his endeavors are less holy-empowered and thus appear as mere badgering and haranguing. In such situations, the Revivalist is little appreciated and much ignored. Some have suggested, however, that these traits are not those of the genuine Revivalist, but rather of a cheap imitator classified under the Charlatan species.

When it comes to the real article, theological explorers will want to take special care with the Revivalist. When he's on, may his numbers increase. When he's off, beware the counterfeit. Overall, few can dispute the Revivalist's unique place in the history of the theological kingdom. Therefore explorers do well to spend some time observing him in his natural habitat. And as one well-known Revivalist exponent has said, "If you're with a bus or a group, they will wait."[3]

---

[1] A complete look at this remarkable fruit is found in Jonathan Edwords's *Grapes of Wrath: Food for Thought With the Revivalist.*

[2] See George Don't-Dallymoore's *Rise and Shine With the Revivalist: A Lengthy Look at the Whitfield Variety.*

[3] For a positive account of the Revivalist, see Bully Sundy's classic *Holy Cries and Happy Howlin': Eyewitness Accounts of Jungle Behavior.*

# The Nihilist
## *(Hole lotta' Nada)*

One of the few creatures indigenous to the Despairing Deserts of the Secular Wastelands is the dark-hearted Nihilist. Though numerous sightings of him have been reported, most of these involve smaller species of Existentialists.

Little is known of the Nihilist's behavior and habitat owing largely to his nocturnal and obtuse nature. He is thought to feed on the shriveled and dry roots of Emptiness and Nothingness that are abundant in this region.

His extremely dark and melancholic markings have made him legend to various Societies of Lost Souls. This repulsive exterior had caused some to believe that he was fierce and extremely dangerous. However, recent evidence shows that he is but a mournful and pathetic creature that threatens only the most aimless of explorers. At no time is this more evident than at night when this sorrowful animal's despairing cries can be heard throughout the haunted wasteland.

Those who have ventured into the emptiness surrounding the Nihilist have concluded that there is absolutely no hope in developing this God-forsaken region. Rather, they tell us that this place may be the infamous location of hell on earth.[1]

---

[1]For further reading on this loathsome loner, see Al B. Damm's depressing text *The Nihilist: A Zero Without a Rim*, vol. 1, Black Hole Press. The second volume, *Ahh, What's the Point*, was abandoned due to lack of interest.

# The M.Div.
## (Puttus Hubbae Thru)

For the past century, theological explorers have generally agreed that the most domesticated and dependable of all the creatures in the lands of the Kingdom Come is the unassuming M.Div. A no-nonsense beast bred to carry the load of theological travelers, the M.Div. is also famous for her hearty appetite. Although known to consume vast amounts of time, money, and sanity, the mainstay of her diet consists of Heavy-Coursework Camellias, Paperwriting Periwinkle, and Read-Everything Rye Grass. The nutrients in these foods make her particularly well suited for ascending the steep slopes of the Seminary Steppes. Properly fed, the M.Div. is commonly considered the only means of mounting a serious expedition into the ominous and forboding Pastoral Plateaus.

More recently, a new movement among experienced travelers has called into question the stamina of the M.Div. for ecclesiastical exploration. The concern of these designer-type explorers pertains to whether this once steady steed is capable of keeping up with the treacherous and changing trails of the Pastorals. There is also doubt whether the kinds of theological supplies the M.Div. carries are adequate for serving the rough-and-ready needs of everyday explorers.[1]

Despite this current trend, most travelers fear that without the M.Div. they stand little chance of reaching the lofty regions of the Pulpit Pinnacle. Of course, any wise explorer ultimately realizes that the means of conquering his Pastoral problems does not depend on the M.Div. alone. Success primarily rests on the traveler's own gritty giftedness and chiseled character.[2] Whatever the case, if this old gray nag ain't what she used to be, it's not for lack of a proud though sometimes disillusioned owner.[3]

---

[1]For an example of this current trend, see I. M. Called's interesting work *Heading the Herds With a Horse of a Different Color.*

[2]Some also consider dumb luck a viable means.

[3]For a standard defense of the M.Div.'s usefulness, see Walter Kizer's *The M.Div.: Packing Into the Pulpits on the Inside Track.*